THE HISTORY OF BRAZIL

History Book 4th Grade Children's Latin American History

BABY PROFESSOR

EDUCATION KIDS

Speedy Publishing LLC

40 E. Main St. #1156

Newark, DE 19711

www.speedypublishing.com

Copyright 2017

Brazil is a large country in South America, stretching from the Amazon Basin north to vineyards and the great Iguacu Falls to the south.

Copacabana Beach

Rio de Janeiro is known for its Copacabana and Ipanema beaches and the raucous, enormous Carnaval festival, including samba music and dance, flamboyant costumes, and a parade of floats. Rio de Janeiro is also known for its 38m Christ the Redeemer statute on top of Munt Corcovado.

Brazil is somewhat smaller than the United States and borders Argentina, Bolivia, Columbia, French Guiana, Guyana, Paraguay, Peru, Suriname, Uruguay, and Venezuela, as well as the Atlantic Ocean.

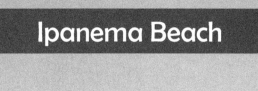
Ipanema Beach

Kaiapos Tribe

HISTORY

Before the Europeans arrived, Brazil had been settled by thousands of smaller tribes. Since these tribes had no writing skills or monumental architecture, there is not much known about them prior to 1500 CE.

COLONIZATION

On April 22, 1500, with the arrival of Pedro Alvares Cabral, who commanded the Portuguese fleet, the land now known as Brazil had been claimed for this Portuguese Empire. Then encountered indigenous peoples that were separated into many tribes, speaking the language of Tupi-Guarani family, and they fought amongst themselves. Even though the original settlement was discovered in 1532, the colonization effectively was started in 1532, as King Dom João III of Portugal divided this territory into 15 independent and private Captaincy Colonies of Brazil.

Pedro Alvares Cabral

Dom João III

However, the unorganized and decentralized tendencies of these colonies were problematic, so, in 1549, the King of Portugal restructured the colonies and created the Governorate General of Brazil, which became a centralized and single Portuguese colony.

During the original two centuries of this colonization, the European and Indigenous groups were constantly at war, creating opportunistic alliance so they could gain the advantage over each other.

Rio de Janeiro

Sugar Cane Plantation

During the mid-16th century, cane sugar became Brazil's best exportation item, and the slaves bought in Sub-Saharan Africa, at the Western Africa slave market, became its greatest import, to cope with the sugarcane plantations, due to the increasing demand internationally for their sugar.

As the end of the 17th century was coming to an end, the sugarcane exports started to decline. In the 1690s, bandeirantes discovered gold which became the new mainstay of their economy, which promoted a Brazilian Gold Rush, attracting thousands from Portugal to Brazil. This led to the increase in the level of immigration which caused conflicts between the old colonies and the newcomers.

Bandeirantes

Prince Regent João

UNITED KINGDOM AND PORTUGAL

The Napoleonic and Spanish forces, during late 1807, threatened continental Portugal's security, which caused Prince Regent João, in Queen Mary I's name, to relocate the royal court from Lisbon to Brazil.

They were able to establish some of Brazil's original financial institutions, like their local stock exchanges, and the National Bank, as well as bringing to an end the monopoly of the Portuguese regarding Brazilian trade and opening Brazil up to additional nations. As retribution for being forced into exile, in 1809 the Prince Regent then organized the Portuguese defeat of French Guiana.

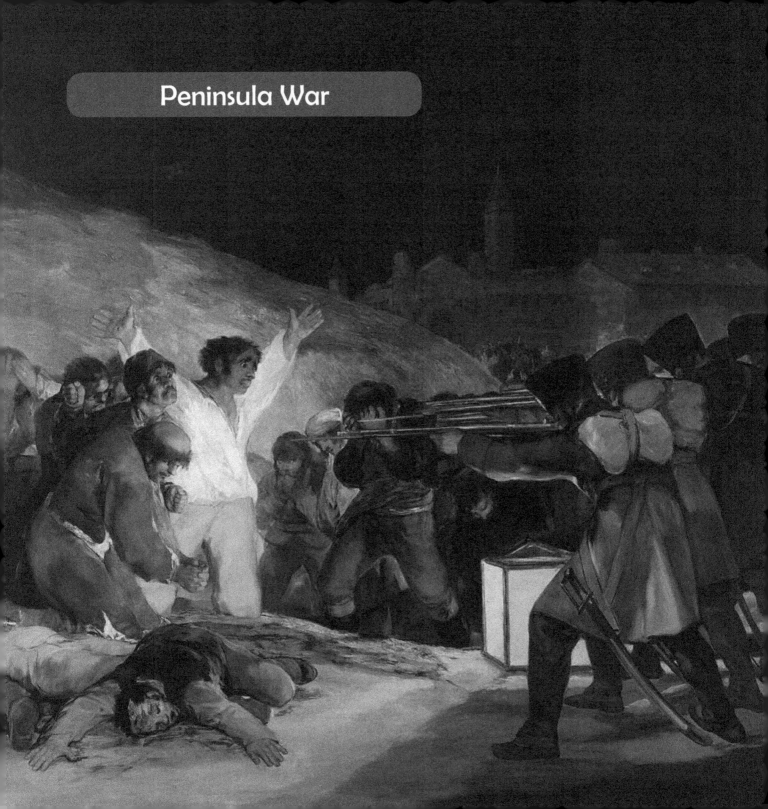

In 1814, at the end of the Peninsular War, Europe demanded Prince Regent João and Queen Maria I return, claiming it was unfit for the head of the ancient European monarchy to live in a colony. To justify living in Brazil, in 1815, the Crown founded the United Kingdom of Portugal, Brazil, and the Algarves, creating a pluricontinental transatlantic monarchic state.

This ploy did not last since Portugal's leadership was resentful of this new status and continued to require that the court of Lisbon return, as well as Brazilians, who were eager for real and practical changes and demanded a republic and independence, which led to the 1817 Pernambucan Revolt.

Pernambucan Revolution

City of Porto

During 1821, as demanded by the revolutionaries that had taken over the city of Porto, D. João VI was not able to hold out for any longer and left for Lisbon. Once he arrived there, he swore to this new constitution, leaving Prince Pedro de Alcântara, his son, as the Kingdom of Brazil's Regent.

INDEPENDENCE

Tension rose between the Brazilians and the Portuguese attempted to re-establish Brazil a colony. The Brazilians would not yield, and Prince Pedro then decided to side with them and declared their independence from Portugal on September 7, 1822. Prince Pedro was named the Emperor of Brazil a month later, and went on to create the Empire of Brazil.

Prince Pedro

The Brazilian War of Independence proceeded to spread through the northern, northeastern regions, and in the Cisplatina province. Once the last of the Portuguese soldiers surrendered on March 8, 1824, Brazil was officially recognized on August 29, 1825. On April 7, 1831, Pedro I traveled to Portugal to reclaim his daughter's crown, relinquishing the Brazilian throne to his young son and heir who was five years old.

Since the young Emperor had no powers until he was of age, the National Assembly set up a regency. Because of this lack of power, several local rebellions occurred. This time of social and political upheaval, including the Praieira revolt, was finally overcome at the end of the 1840s.

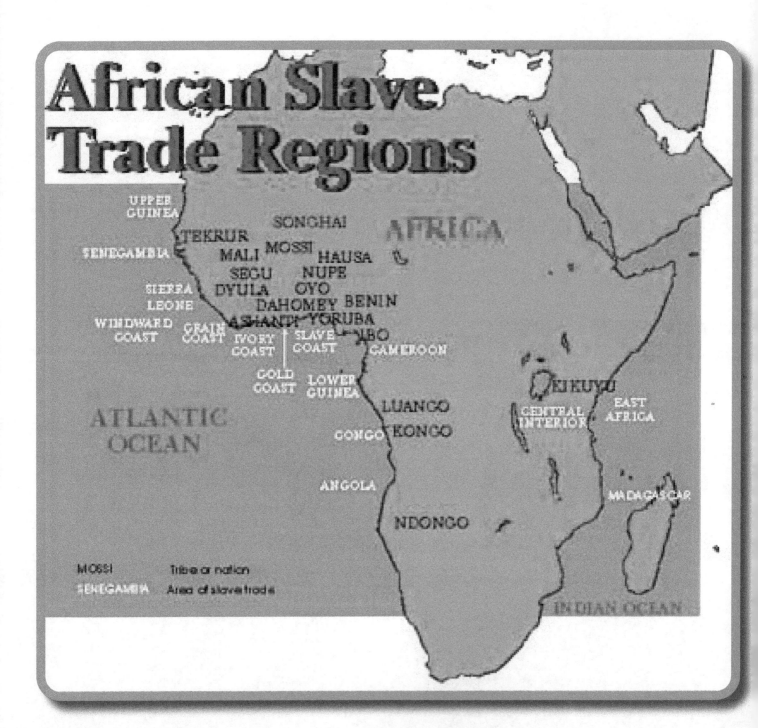

During this monarchy's last phase, the political debate focused on the slavery issue. In 1850, the Atlantic slave trade was vacated resulting from the British Aberdeen Act, only in May of 1888 was the institution officially abolished.

THE EARLY YEARS AS A REPUBLIC

Following two severe catastrophes, economic and military, the republican people gained their power. The cycle of instability created by these two crises damaged the regime, in the wake of his running mate's murder, leading to the Brazilian Revolution of 1930. Getúlio Vargas was only to be in power for a short time, but he closed Congress, terminated the Constitution, used his emergency powers to rule, and replaced the governors with his supporters.

Brazilian Revolution

Getúlio Vargas

There were three attempts in the 1930s to remove Vargas and his supporters. The first failed attempt was known as the Constitutional Revolution of 1932, the second was the Brazilian uprising of 1935 which had been led by the communists, and the third was the Integralist Movement in May of 1938.

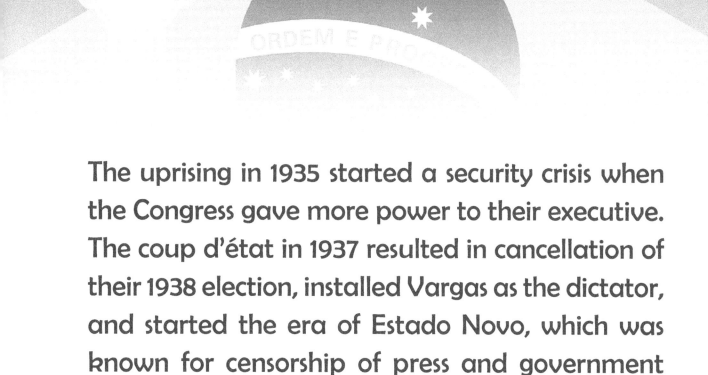

The uprising in 1935 started a security crisis when the Congress gave more power to their executive. The coup d'état in 1937 resulted in cancellation of their 1938 election, installed Vargas as the dictator, and started the era of Estado Novo, which was known for censorship of press and government brutality.

During World War II, Brazil stayed neutral until August of 1942, when they entered with the allies, after retaliations by Fascist Italy and Nazi German, since they had severed relations with Axis powers because of the Pan-American Conference.

World War II

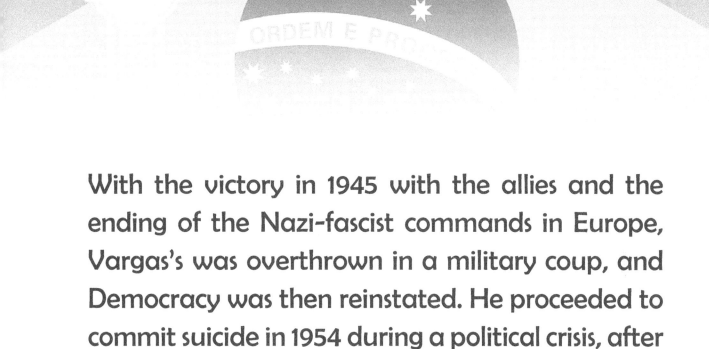

With the victory in 1945 with the allies and the ending of the Nazi-fascist commands in Europe, Vargas's was overthrown in a military coup, and Democracy was then reinstated. He proceeded to commit suicide in 1954 during a political crisis, after returning to power in the election of 1950.

Juscelino Kubitschek

THE CONTEMPORARY ERA

After Vargas's suicide, there were several short-term governments. In 1956, Juscelino Kubitschek became president. The economy and industry sector grew tremendously, but his biggest achievement was construction of the new capital city, Brasília, which was inaugurated in 1960. Jânio Quadros became his successor, but resigned within a year, in 1961.

João Goulart, his vice-president then assumed the presidency, but provoked a strong political opposition and was then deposed by a coup in April 1964, resulting in a military regime.

João Goulart

This regime was only meant to be transitory, but gradually it closed in and then became a dictatorship with promulgation of the Fifth Institutional Act in 1968. In spite of its brutality, as with similar totalitarian governments, due to an economic boom, this regime attained its highest popularity level early in the 1970s.

José Sarney

Once José Sarney became president in 1985, the civilians claimed their power back. He soon became unpopular because of his failure to control the economic disaster and the hyperinflation which had been inherited from the regime. His government, being unsuccessful, allowed Fernando Collor to be elected in 1989, and he was then impeached in 1992 by the National Congress.

He was then succeeded by Itamar Franco, his vice-president, who proceeded to appoint Fernando Henrique Cardoso as the Minister of Finance. Cardoso then, in 1994, produced the very successful Plano Real, which, after many decades of economic plans that had failed, was finally able to stabilize the economy of Brazil, which led to him being elected that year, as well as in 1998.

Itamar Franco

Luiz Inácio Lula da Silva

The transition of power from Henrique to Luiz Inácio Lula da Silva was peaceful and this seemed to be proof that they were finally successful in realizing political stability they sought. However, frustrations and indignation had accumulated and many peaceful protests were held during Dilma Rousseff's first term, who had succeeded Lula. After political and economic crises, having evidence of political involvement, the Brazilian Congress impeached Rousseff in 2016.

For additional information about the history of Brazil, you can go to your local library, research the internet, and ask questions of your teachers, family, and friends.

CPSIA information can be obtained
at www.ICGtesting.com
Printed in the USA
LVHW021146020420
652008LV00018B/1859